love COLLECTION 100%

objects of my affection

loves me not, loves me

Sarah Mugg

objects of my

affection

Sarah Mlugg

**Andrews McMeel
Publishing**

Kansas City

www.andrewsmcmeel.com
www.sarahlugg.com

00 01 02 03 04 TK 10 9 8 7 6 5 4 3 2 1

Library of Congress Catalog Card Number: 00-103143
ISBN: 0-7407-1248-9

Edited by Patrick Regan
Design by Stephanie R. Farley

to my parents

with love

and thanks

List of Illustrations

*M*ake each day
a further exploration
into the depths of your heart.

A book *of* poems, collages, *and* paintings.

I am, without doubt, an incorrigible and true romantic. I profoundly believe in the power of love and the way it brightens our lives. My life and work have taught me that seeing through the eyes of love is a most powerful filter, and I cannot regard the natural world without feeling a deep love for her ingenuity, honesty, energy and pure beauty. I love the unknown—the voyage of discovery embarked upon when taking time out to look at nature's creations.

And her creations inspire my own. My piece, *Out of the Blue*, was inspired by a memorable visit to a secluded beach, Sandwood Bay on the northwest coast of Scotland. I had fallen in love with this beach as a child when I first visited it with my parents and vowed to return as soon as possible—as we all do. Now, many years later, I was returning as a young woman with my partner Robert.

To reach the bay you hike on foot across rugged Highland terrain for about four miles, after which you are rewarded by a beach of stunning pale shell-pink sand bordering a Caribbean-blue sea inhabited by beautifully hued jellyfish. The magic of the place is enhanced by its deserted remoteness. I spent most of the day scouring the beach with my nose just a few inches from the sand and so I was unaware of Robert's activities. Hidden by a dune, he had been writing a proposal of marriage in the sand. When finished, he placed me, eyes closed, directly in front of the huge letters and only then let me open my eyes. When we first arrived at the beach I had been utterly entranced by its perfectly smooth sand with not a single footprint apart from those of the Kittiwakes who danced amongst the tumbling waves. I later found out that these bird footprints are known locally as "messages in the sand." Little did I know that on this beach I would discover my very own message of love in the sand.

Receiving such a lovely message written upon nature's beautiful canvas made it all the more magical, for I love the natural world with all my heart. And my love of nature manifests itself in my work on a daily basis. Sometimes, I'll use a single object—a daisy, seashell or pebble—and at other times, I'll include a delicious amalgam of collected objects taking their theme from nature herself. A walk in the woods, an afternoon's stroll along a sun-kissed beach, the seasons and the colour palette to be found within the treasures themselves send me, wild with delight, scuttling down another route. Whether it is a solitary object within a painting or one of my label assemblages, I feel that they are an homage to the beauty and genius of nature.

My love of nature and art, as well as my personal scribblings, have been well-nurtured by my parents, and I will always be in their debt for this. My mother trained as a painter and then went into textiles so there was always an abundance of art materials and encouragement at home. As my mother puts it, she has always encouraged my "fiddly fingers!"

Like nature, poetry often serves as a creative wellspring for my work. In this book, I've included several writings that have inspired me. When I was only eight years old, I was lucky enough to have a teacher who encouraged us not only to read and illustrate poems but also to write them. I can still remember the first poem I illustrated, *Ode to Autumn* by Keats. It shone a new light on what, up until then, I had thought boring!

I haven't written a poem for a long time now, but I often include favorite little snippets in my artwork—written thoughts to complement my visual ones. These words are often composed of individual letters cut out of a book my mother gave me when I was working on a series of pieces inspired by a trip to northern Tuscany. The book, a compilation of poems by Byron which she had had at school, was very appropriate at the time as he and Shelley had stayed very near to where we had been on holiday.

Many of the poems collected here are very personal to me, including the ones read at our wedding and a few family favourites such as *Come into the Garden Maud* by Tennyson. I don't think anyone in our family can read this without picturing my grandfather stepping out into his conservatory with its blue glass stars, its huge blue and white Chinese pots, and the blue plumbago (in my mind always flowering, of course!). He was a great lover of Tennyson and of his garden. So whenever anyone suggested he might come into the garden, the rest would follow without fail!

The poets I admire turned the mundane into something sublime. I feel a kinship with them as I often take simple, humble objects from nature, place them in a new context, and find people in complete awe at the result. Taking things out of context lets them be seen in a fresh light and helps reveal their inherent beauty that we busy humans too often miss. Seeing the natural world this way is not hard to do—one only has to remember to look through the eyes of love.

I hope this collection of poems and art makes your heart sing.

Sarah Nugg

Here are fruits,
flowers,
leaves and branches,

And here is my
which beats only for you.

—*Paul Verlaine*

$\mathcal{O}$ tender yearning, sweet hoping!

The golden time of first love!

The eye sees the open heaven,

The heart is intoxicated with bliss;

O that the beautiful time of young love

Could remain GREEN forever.

—*Johann Christoph Friedrich von Schiller,* The Song of the Bell

Come into the garden, Maud

For the black bat, night, has flown,

Come into the garden, Maud,

I am here at the gate alone;

And the woodbine spices are wafted abroad,

And the musk of the rose is blown.

For a breeze of morning moves,

And the planet of Love is on high,

Beginning to faint in the light that she loves

On a bed of daffodil sky,

To faint in the light of the sun she loves,

To faint in his light, and to die.

—*Alfred, Lord Tennyson*

if I keep a green
bough in my
the singing bird
will come

For lo, the winter is past,

the rain is over and gone;

The flowers appear on the earth;

the time of the singing of the birds is come,

and the voice of the turtle

is heard in our land;

The fig tree putteth forth her green figs,

and the vines with the tender grape

give a good smell.

Arise, my love, my fair one,

and come away.

—*The Song of Solomon*

A virgin purest lipp'd,

yet in the lore

Of love deep learned

to the red heart's core.

—John Keats

I am certain of nothing but of the holiness of the HEART'S affections

and the truth of Imagination—

What the imagination seizes as BEAUTY must be truth—

whether it existed before or not.

—John Keats

listen to your
heart, believe
in yourself
trust in your
instincts.......

new MESSAGES

For winter's rains and ruins are over,

And all the season of snows and sins;

The day dividing lover and lover,

The light that loses, the night that wins;

And time remembered is grief forgotten,

And frosts are slain and flowers begotten,

And in green underwood and cover

Blossom by blossom the spring begins.

—*Algernon Charles Swinburne*,
Atalanta in Calydon

We find great things
are made of little things,
And little things
go lessening till at last
Comes God behind them.
—*Robert Browning*

The human heart
has hidden treasures,
In secret kept,
in silence sealed.
—*Charlotte Brontë*, Evening Solace

*B*eyond a mortal man impassion'd far

At these voluptuous accents, he arose,

Ethereal, flush'd, and like a throbbing star

Seen mid the sapphire heaven's deep repose;

Into her dream he melted, as the rose,

Blendeth its odour with the violet,—

Solution sweet: meantime the frost-wind blows

Like Love's alarum pattering the sharp sleet

Against the window-panes; St. Agnes' moon hath set.

—*John Keats,* The Eve of St. Agnes

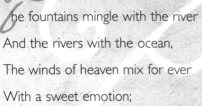

The fountains mingle with the river
And the rivers with the ocean,
The winds of heaven mix for ever
With a sweet emotion;

Nothing in the world is single,
All things by a law divine
In one another's being mingle—
Why not I with thine?

See the mountains kiss high heaven
And the waves clasp one another;
No sister-flower would be forgiven
If it disdain'd its brother.

And the sunlight clasps the earth,
And the moonbeams kiss the sea—
What are all these kissings worth,
If thou kiss not me?

—*Percy Bysshe Shelley*

Come live with me, and be my love,

And we will some new pleasures prove

Of golden sands, and crystal brooks,

With silken lines, and silver hooks.

—*John Donne,* The Bait

$\mathscr{E}$verything that grows

Holds in perfection but a little moment.

-Shakespeare, Sonnet 15

The world stands out on either side

No wider than the heart is wide;

Above the world is stretched the sky,—

No higher than the soul is high.

The heart can push the sea and land

Farther away on either hand;

The world can split the sky in two,

And let the face of God shine through.

But East and West will pinch the heart

That cannot keep them pushed apart;

And he whose soul is flat—the sky

Will cave in on him by and by.

—*Edna St. Vincent Millay*

She Walks in Beauty, like the night
Of cloudless climes and starry skies;
And all that's best of dark and bright
Meet in her aspect and her eyes:
Thus mellow'd to that tender light
Which heaven to gaudy day denies.

One shade the more, one ray the less,
Had half impair'd the nameless grace
Which waves in every raven tress,
Or softly lightens o'er her face;
Where thoughts serenely sweet express
How pure, how dear their dwelling-place.

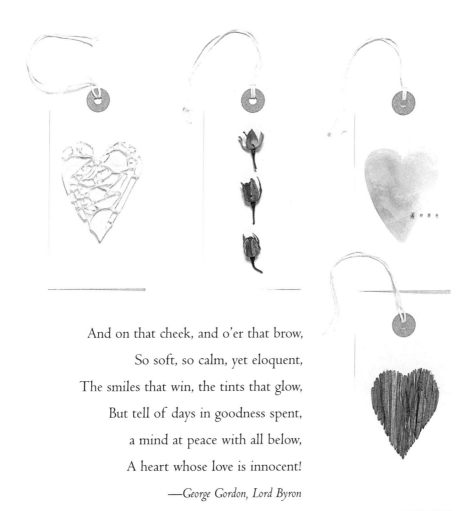

And on that cheek, and o'er that brow,

So soft, so calm, yet eloquent,

The smiles that win, the tints that glow,

But tell of days in goodness spent,

a mind at peace with all below,

A heart whose love is innocent!

—*George Gordon, Lord Byron*

Shall I compare thee to a summer's day?
Thou art more lovely and more temperate:
Rough winds do shake the darling buds of May,
And summer's lease hath all too short a date:
Sometime too hot the eye of heaven shines,
And often is his gold complexion dimm'd,
And every fair from fair sometime declines,
By chance or nature's changing course untrimm'd:
But thy eternal summer shall not fade,
Nor lose possession of that fair thou owest,
Nor shall death brag thou wander'st in his shade,
When in eternal lines to time thou growest,
So long as men can breathe or eyes can see,
So long lives this, and this gives life to thee.

—*William Shakespeare,* Sonnet 18

amour

LOVE

Golden head by golden head,
Like two pigeons in one nest
Folded in each other's wings,
They lay down in their curtained bed.
Like two blossoms on one stem,
Like two flakes of new-fall'n snow,
Like two wands of ivory
Tipped with gold for awful kings.

Laura and

Believe

Lizzie Asleep

Moon and stars gazed in at them,

Wind sang to them lullaby

Lumbering owls forbore to fly,

Not a bat flapped to and fro

Round their nest:

Cheek to cheek and breast to breast

Locked together in one nest.

—*Christina G. Rossetti*

The red rose whispers of passion

And the white rose breathes of love;

O, the red rose is a falcon,

And the white rose is a dove.

—*John Boyle O'Reilly,* A White Rose

O my luve's like a red, red rose,

That's newly sprung in June;

O my luve's like the melodie

That's sweetly play'd in tune.

—*Robert Burns,* A Red, Red Rose

Red Rose

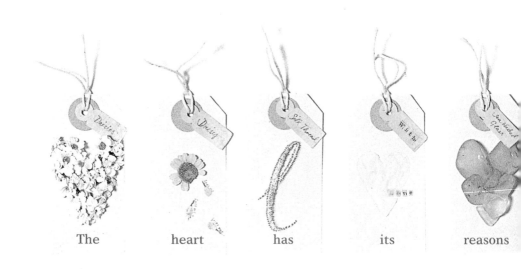

The   heart   has   its   reasons

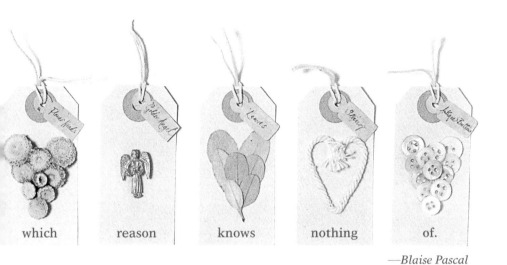

which   reason   knows   nothing   of.

—*Blaise Pascal*

*T*wice or thrice had I loved thee,

Before I knew thy face or name.

—*John Donne,* Air and Angels

i f ever thou shalt love,

In the sweet pangs of it remember me;

For such as I am all true lovers are:

Unstaid and skittish in all motions else

Save in the constant image of the creature

That is belov'd.

——*William Shakespeare,* Twelfth-Night

Unlearn'd, he knew
no schoolman's subtle art,
No language, but the language
of the heart.

—*Alexander Pope*

*T*o wake the soul by tender strokes of art,

To raise the genius, and to mend the heart;

To make mankind, in conscious virtue bold,

Live o'er each scene, and be what they behold:

For this the Tragic Muse first trod the stage.

—*Alexander Pope,* Prologue to Mr. Addison's Cato

The HOLIEST of all HOLIDAYS are those

Kept by ourselves in silence and apart;

The secret ANNIVERSARIES of the HEART.

—*Henry Wadsworth Longfellow*

50

So we grew together,

Like to a double cherry, seeming parted,

But yet an union in partition;

Two lovely berries molded on one stem.

—*William Shakespeare,* A Midsummer-Night's Dream

Sonnet from the Portuguese XIV

If thou must love me, let it be for nought
Except for love's sake only. Do not say
'I love her for her smile . . . her look . . . her way
Of speaking gently . . . for a trick of thought
That falls in well with mine, and certes brought
A sense of pleasant ease on such a day'—
For these things in themselves, Beloved, may
Be changed, or change for thee,—and love, so wrought,
May be unwrought so. Neither love me for
Thine own dear pity's wiping my cheeks dry,
Since one might well forget to weep who bore
Thy comfort long, and lose thy love thereby.
But love me for love's sake, that evermore
Thou may'st love on through love's eternity.

—*Elizabeth Barrett Browning*

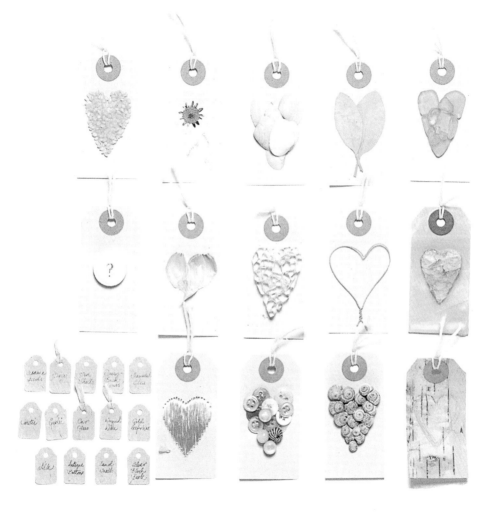

Give all to love;
Obey thy HEART;
Friends, kindred, days,
Estate, good fame,
Plans, credit and the Muse,
Nothing refuse.

—*Ralph Waldo Emerson*

*O*ur HEART is a treasury;
if you spend all its wealth at once you are ruined.
We find it as difficult to forgive a person for displaying his feeling
in all its nakedness as we do to forgive a man for being penniless.

—*Honore de Balzac*

The Passionate Shepherd to his Love

Come live with me and be my Love,

And we will all the pleasures prove,

That hills and valleys, dale and field,

And all the craggy mountains yield.

—*Christopher Marlow*

But to see her was to love her,

Love but her, and love forever.

Had we never lov'd sae kindly,

Had we never lov'd sae blindly,

Never met—or never parted—

We had na'er been brokenhearted.

—*Robert Burns*

The golden hours
        on angel wings
Flew o'er me
       and my dearie;
For dear to me
       as light and life
Was my sweet
       Highland Mary.
          —*Robert Burns*

When You Are Old

When you are old and grey and full of sleep,
And nodding by the fire, take down this book,
And slowly read, and dream of the soft look
Your eye's had once, and of their shadows deep;

How many loved your moments of glad grace,
And loved your beauty with love false or true,
But one man loved the pilgrim soul in you,
And loved the sorrows of your changing face;

And bending down beside the glowing bars,
Murmur, a little sadly, how Love fled
And paced upon the mountains overhead
And hid its face amid a crowd of stars.

—*William Butler Yeats*

ours fly
        Flowers die.
New days,
        New ways
    Pass by;
        Love stays.

—*Henry Van Dyke*

62

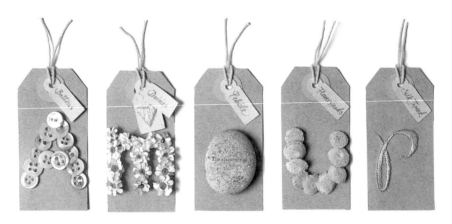

Viva l'amour!